ideals THANKSGIVING

W9-AMW-732

Thanksgiving is a time
for remembering
The good gifts of every day,
The countless blessings that
are ever ours
As we go along the way.

Thanksgiving is a time for
remembering
And each time this day draws
near,
The hearts of mankind join in
grateful praise
At this special time of year.

Virginia Katherine Oliver

Publisher, Patricia A. Pingry
Editor, Ramona Richards
Art Director, David Lenz
Permissions, Kathleen Gilbert
Copy Editor, Peggy Schaefer
Phototypesetter, Tammy Walsh
Publicity, Carol Wedekind

ISBN 0-8249-1047-8

IDEALS—Vol. 43, No. 7 November MCMLXXXVI IDEALS (ISSN 0019-137X) is published eight times a year,
February, March, May, June, August, September, November, December
by IDEALS PUBLISHING CORPORATION, Nelson Place at Elm Hill Pike, Nashville, Tenn. 37214-8000
Second class postage paid at Nashville, Tennessee, and additional mailing offices.
Copyright © MCMLXXXVI by IDEALS PUBLISHING CORPORATION.
POSTMASTER: Send address changes to Ideals, Post Office Box 148000, Nashville, Tenn. 37214-8000
All rights reserved. Title IDEALS registered U.S. Patent Office.
Published simultaneously in Canada.

SINGLE ISSUE—$3.50
ONE-YEAR SUBSCRIPTION—eight consecutive issues as published—$15.95
TWO-YEAR SUBSCRIPTION—sixteen consecutive issues as published—$27.95
Outside U.S.A., add $4.00 per subscription year for postage and handling.

The cover and entire contents of IDEALS are fully protected by copyright and must
not be reproduced in any manner whatsoever. Printed and bound in U.S.A.
by The Banta Co., Menasha, Wisconsin.

Front and back covers by Fred Sieb
Inside front cover by Fred Sieb
Inside back cover by John Vondell

Harvest and Thanksgiving Time

I see a harvest moon tonight,
Though it's Thanksgiving time;
Its golden beams are shining still
On woodlands' towering pines.
It shines upon the empty fields
Which have been harvested
And sheds a special ray of light
Upon the old homestead.

Again I see a harvest moon,
Though it's Thanksgiving time;
I feel a surge of thankfulness
Within this heart of mine.
The gathered fruit, heads bowed in prayer...
Where's one, we find the other;
For harvest and Thanksgiving time
Are kin to one another.

Loise Pinkerton Fritz

Photo Opposite
FALL HARVEST
Fred Sieb

Harvest Call

The wheat is cut, a bumper yield,
And sunshine falls upon the field
Of stubble, yellow as spun gold,
Where bales of straw lay tightly rolled.

The cricket sings among the weeds,
And tree frogs pipe from slender reeds.
Red clover, wet with dew at dawn,
Tells of a harvest come and gone.

So short the time from blossomed spring
Till combines hum and sickles sing;
So short a time from spring to fall,
To the end of work and the harvest call.

Dan A. Hoover

Autumn Morn

I like to watch as autumn's morn
Casts shadows through the yellow corn
And silhouettes the apple tree
Where branches low hold fruit for me.
My garden that I coaxed to grow
Is staging now its final show,
While on the hillside gold and red,
The earth prepares its winter bed.

Small creatures rush about to hide
The food that nature has supplied,
And blue skies watch for birds a-wing
That must escape earth's slumbering.
The glow that's seen across the land
Reveals perfection as God planned,
And autumn's morn becomes for me
A lesson in fine artistry!

Gertrude Dicks

Fall Colors

Jack Frost has painted a colorful scene.
  Only the pines and fir stay green.
Oak leaves of red and golden maple leaves
  Dance gaily by on the gentle breeze.

Walnut trees think yellow leaves are proper
  While the mountain ash has leaves of copper.
The rust-colored leaves of the chestnut trees
  And the orange shellbark leaves
  float down with ease.

The poplar and birch leaves have changed to gold.
  The colors are all so bright and so bold.
Leaves are falling everywhere you look,
  Making tiny boats on the rippling brook.

Fall is the brightest time of the year.
  Jack Frost is telling you that winter is near.

Mary Ann Schaeffer

Photo Opposite
FALL COLORS IN
ONEONTA, NY
Stephen Parker

Country Chronicle

Thanksgiving is a festive day indoors and out. Families gather around teeming tables to express heartfelt thanks for what the land has yielded in its season of fruition. Though the hills are brown and sere, for those who follow the wonders of nature, there is a loveliness that brightens the holiday with lingering hues of red and gold.

On thin hillsides and in abandoned fields, after the rusty golden leaves of witch hazel have fluttered to the ground, the small trees are filled with yellow blooms which spread out feathery and ribbon-like among slender boughs. Seed pods of a year ago still cling to the branches, ready to explode with such force that the nuts are scattered many feet from the tree.

Some of the dandelions lift up their bowls of gold, defying frost and freeze as they reach for sunlight deep in the grass. The clustered orange berries of bittersweet cover the vines that twist and twine as they cling to old stone walls. Chickweed shows its tiny stars of white in the garden's edge.

In swamps and marshes, the bright red berries of black alder, a member of the holly family, spread splendor against a background of withered fields that reach up into the hills from a gentle stream flowing among the reeds and cattails. There, in the channel of the sluggish waters, musk-rats build their houses of mud and sticks and roots.

Alder berries set the swamp aglow in cloud or sun. Often glazed in ice from freezing rains, the berries in their silvered sheen shine and glow, cheering and warming the heart and spirit of a walker by the shore.

Nature helps light the way to a deeper understanding of harvest's end and of what God has given to humankind. We sing our praises of gratitude for His providence, for the goodness of the seasons, and for home and hills.

Thanksgiving Day is one of the last stepping stones from autumn into a wondrous world of white when the earth takes its winter of rest under snow. Nature is like a mother tucking her child under the blankets when bedtime falls. And late November, with shortened hours of sunlight, turns the lamps low, and the land begins a long night of sleep.

Lansing Christman

Feels Like Fall

The shorter days have
    changed our phase.
I bid you look around.
The nights so cool make
    mornings drool
Upon the thirsty ground.
Small bits of red and
    orange are fed
Into the leafy trees.
Birdlife expands to fly in
    bands
Against a southern
    breeze.

The people call, "It feels
    like fall!"
And we return the shout,
As spiders spin and
    webs begin
To round the corners
    out.
The squirrels race with
    nut-filled faces
To fend the winter clime,
Or is their goal to dig a
    hole
To bury summertime?

Margaret Rorke

AUTUMN IN THE MOUNTAINS
Wesley Walden

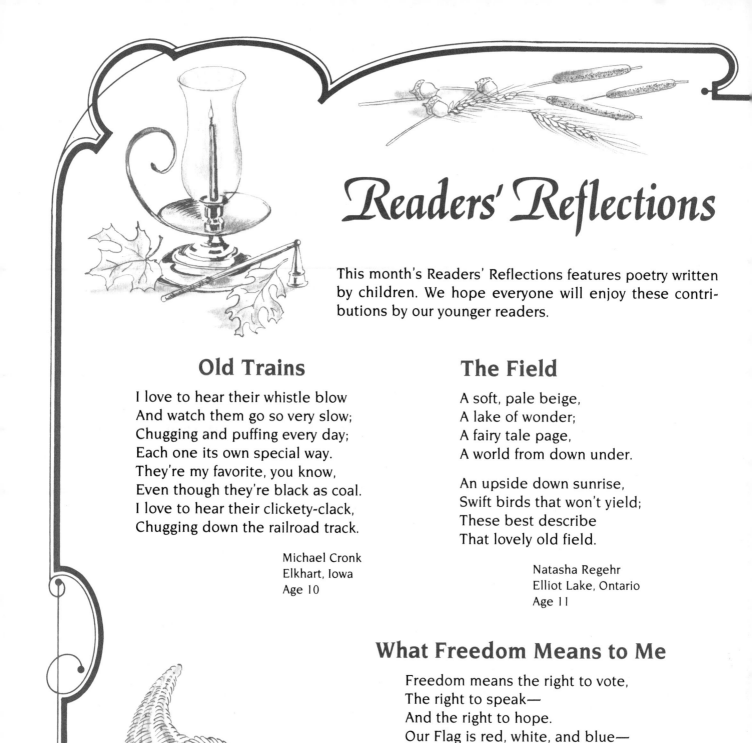

Readers' Reflections

This month's Readers' Reflections features poetry written by children. We hope everyone will enjoy these contributions by our younger readers.

Old Trains

I love to hear their whistle blow
And watch them go so very slow;
Chugging and puffing every day;
Each one its own special way.
They're my favorite, you know,
Even though they're black as coal.
I love to hear their clickety-clack,
Chugging down the railroad track.

Michael Cronk
Elkhart, Iowa
Age 10

The Field

A soft, pale beige,
A lake of wonder;
A fairy tale page,
A world from down under.

An upside down sunrise,
Swift birds that won't yield;
These best describe
That lovely old field.

Natasha Regehr
Elliot Lake, Ontario
Age 11

What Freedom Means to Me

Freedom means the right to vote,
The right to speak—
And the right to hope.
Our Flag is red, white, and blue—
Its colors fly high and true.
We are blessed one and all,
To have a country proud and tall.

Cassandra Dee Johnson
Leavenworth, WA
Age 10

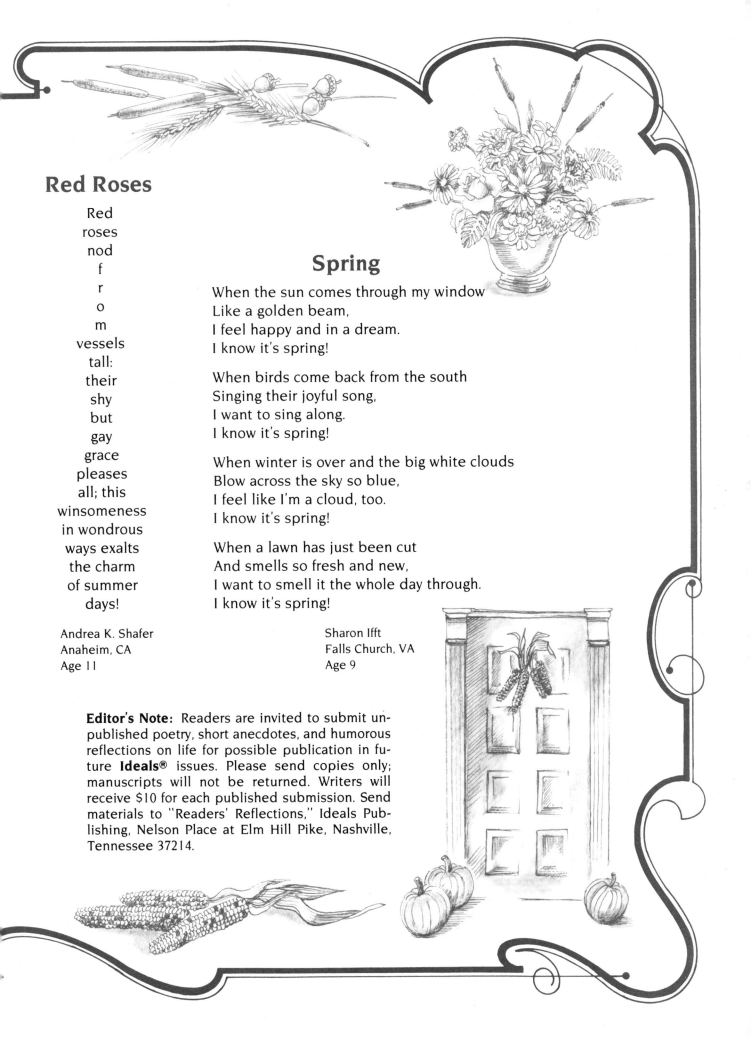

Red Roses

Red
roses
nod
f
r
o
m
vessels
tall:
their
shy
but
gay
grace
pleases
all; this
winsomeness
in wondrous
ways exalts
the charm
of summer
days!

Andrea K. Shafer
Anaheim, CA
Age 11

Spring

When the sun comes through my window
Like a golden beam,
I feel happy and in a dream.
I know it's spring!

When birds come back from the south
Singing their joyful song,
I want to sing along.
I know it's spring!

When winter is over and the big white clouds
Blow across the sky so blue,
I feel like I'm a cloud, too.
I know it's spring!

When a lawn has just been cut
And smells so fresh and new,
I want to smell it the whole day through.
I know it's spring!

Sharon Ifft
Falls Church, VA
Age 9

Editor's Note: Readers are invited to submit unpublished poetry, short anecdotes, and humorous reflections on life for possible publication in future **Ideals®** issues. Please send copies only; manuscripts will not be returned. Writers will receive $10 for each published submission. Send materials to "Readers' Reflections," Ideals Publishing, Nelson Place at Elm Hill Pike, Nashville, Tennessee 37214.

Fairy Ships

When mother tells me that I may,
I go for little walks each day.
Sometimes I tarry by the stream
To watch the falling leaves and dream.

I fancy they are fairy ships
That sail away on magic trips—
To gather riches from afar,
Where gold and silk and spices are.

I see their tiny, shiny sails
That rise and fall upon the gales.
And there upon the deck she stands—
A Fairy Queen with outstretched hands.

She calls to me so soft and low,
I wonder, should I—dare I go?
I near the ship but all in vain,
Alas, it's just a leaf again!

Kirstin

Photo Opposite
AU SABLE FALLS
Grand Marais, MI
Ray Elliott

Thanksgiving Desserts

Basic Pie Crust

2 cups all-purpose flour
½ teaspoon salt
⅔ cup shortening
6 tablespoons ice water

Sift flour and salt together. Cut in shortening with a pastry blender until mixture resembles coarse cornmeal. Add ice water by the tablespoonful until mixture holds together. Roll out on a floured board. Makes pastry for 1 double-crust 9-inch pie.

Note: To keep pie crust from getting soggy, before filling, brush sides and bottom of crust with beaten egg white. Bake in a preheated 375° oven for about 4 minutes. Then fill and bake as directed in recipe.

Cranberry Pie

1 pound fresh cranberries
1 6½-ounce can pineapple chunks, drained
1 cup pineapple juice
2 cups sugar
2 tablespoons unflavored gelatin
  Juice of 1 lemon
1 9-inch pie shell, baked
  Whipped cream
  Chopped nuts

Combine first 6 ingredients in a saucepan; bring to a boil. Heat for 10 minutes, stirring frequently; set aside to cool for 15 minutes. Pour mixture into pie shell; chill until firm. Spread with whipped cream and sprinkle with chopped nuts before serving.

Apple Caramel Pie

6 apples, peeled, cored, and sliced
1 unbaked 9-inch deep-dish pie shell
½ cup butter at room temperature
½ cup flour
1½ cups firmly packed brown sugar
¼ teaspoon salt
2¼ teaspoons cinnamon
1 cup chopped walnuts
  Whipped cream

Preheat oven to 350°. Arrange apple slices in pie shell. Combine butter, flour, brown sugar, salt, and cinnamon in a bowl. Spread mixture over apples; sprinkle with walnuts. Bake for 50 minutes. Serve with whipped cream.

Sour Cream Fruit Pie

½ cup fruit juice
2 cups mixed fruit (bananas, green grapes, strawberries *or* canned pineapple, sliced and drained)
½ cup firmly packed brown sugar
1 3-ounce package of lime or lemon gelatin
1 cup sour cream
1 9-inch pie shell, baked
  Whipped cream
  Nuts

Pour juice over bananas to keep them from turning dark; set aside for 15 minutes. Drain bananas, pouring juice into a saucepan. Add brown sugar to juice and bring to a boil, stirring until sugar is dissolved. Stir in gelatin until dissolved. Remove from heat; cool for 15 minutes. Fold in sour cream and fruit. Pour into pie shell and chill until firm. Cover with whipped cream and sprinkle with nuts before serving.

Photo Opposite
CRANBERRY PIE
Gerald Koser

The Original Thanksgiving Meal

Our harvest being gotten in, our Governor sente four men out fowling that so we might, after a more special manner, rejoyce together after we had gathered the fruit of our labours. These four, in one day, killed as much fowl as, with a little help besides, served the company almost a week, at which time, amongst other recreations, we exercised our armes, many of the Indians coming amongst us.

And amongst the rest, their greatest King, Massasoit, with some ninety men, whom, for three days, we entertained and feasted.

And they went out and killed five deer, which they brought to the Plantation, and bestowed on our Governor and upon the Captaine and others.

And although it be not always so plentiful as it was at this time with us, yet, by the goodness of God, we are so farr from wante that we often wish you partakers of our plentie.

~Edward Winslow
Plymouth, Massachusetts, 1621
A Letter to England

What was the first Thanksgiving really like? It is surprising to learn that although many of our traditional Thanksgiving dishes are associated with the Pilgrims, most of these foods were not actually present at the original Thanksgiving meal. In fact, the entire Thanksgiving feast has changed substantially as it evolved into the holiday we now celebrate.

History tells us that the original celebration lasted three days. Although the actual dates of the festival were never recorded, most historians agree that the event took place in October rather than November.

The occasion was an outdoor event, celebrated during one of New England's mild Indian Summers. Sporting events such as shooting contests and other recreations were held between meals. The cooking was done on open spits and in outdoor ovens. Tables were made by placing long boards over sawhorses. Chairs consisted of stools and tree stumps. Eating utensils consisted primarily of pewter dishes, wooden bowls, knives, and spoons. (Forks were not commonly used during the seventeenth century.)

Because the feasting lasted for three days, a large number of ingredients went into the meals to add variety. They did not spend the last two days eating turkey leftovers! What they did and did not eat may come as a revelation.

Contrary to common belief, turkey was probably not the main meat dish at the first Thanksgiving. Turkeys are not specifically mentioned in the feast records; however, prior to the celebration, Governor Bradford had sent out four men to go fowling. The records state that "these four, in one day, killed as much fowl as served the company almost a week." We can assume that turkeys were among the birds killed as they were very plentiful in the region. The Pilgrims had taken in a "great store of wild Turkies" during the summer. However, roast duck and goose must also be added to the list of original ingredients in the first Thanksgiving meal

as we also have records of these fowl being plentiful.

Perhaps the largest single meat dish was venison, as Chief Massasoit and his braves brought five deer to the feast for their contribution to the meal. Other meats at the banqueting table included striped bass, cod, clams and other shellfish, lobster, and eel. With such a wide array of meats, twentieth century cooks can choose from a large selection of main dishes and still serve what could technically be called a "traditional" Thanksgiving meal!

Both Old and New World vegetables provided a delightful mixture to the first menu. These included beans, pumpkins, squash, turnips, parsnips, barley, onions, leeks, watercress and other "sallet herbes," and roasted Indian corn (the colorful variety we now hang on our doors and lampposts in autumn). A small amount of peas may also have been included. (Unfortunately, the pea crop had largely failed that year. Letters to England reveal that despite an abundant corn harvest, "the peas (were) not worth gathering, for we feared they were too late sown. They came up very well and blossomed, but the sun parched them in the blossom.")

White and dark breads were served with butter during the feast. The white bread consisted of leftover ship biscuit (and butter) from the **Mayflower.** The dark bread was made of cornmeal, barley, and rye flour. It was called "Rye and Injun" and was very nutritious. It soon became the common bread of the early colonists.

Wild fruits grew in abundance in the American wilderness. Among those fruits that graced the first Thanksgiving table were wild plums and dried berries such as wild blueberries, blackberries, raspberries, and strawberries. A popular misconception is that the Pilgrims also ate cranberries. Although neighboring bogs were full of them, there is no historical evidence that the Pilgrims ever learned to make use of the red fruit that would later become one of the area's leading industries.

Fruits served as the primary dessert fare on the original Thanksgiving menu. There is a good chance, however, that hasty pudding or Indian pudding made from cornmeal was also served. Pumpkin pie, that all-American favorite Thanksgiving dessert, had not yet been invented. In the early days, the Pilgrims stewed their pumpkins and served it as a sauce. Their only pies were English-style meat pies. References indicate that succulent eel pie was among the items served during the original feast.

The three day celebration was such a great success, that it was held again in subsequent years. The tradition spread and was carried on sporadically until 1863 when President Lincoln designated a national Thanksgiving Day. With its early origins on the shores of the American wilderness, it is certainly the oldest and most distinctively American holiday that we celebrate as a people.

James W. Hyland III

Speechless

Where pale mists wreathed a purple hill
At edge of evening, rapt and still,
I heard a dark crow's raucous cry
Tear ragged edges in the sky.

A bird, bright blue beyond belief,
Boldly proclaimed someone a thief.
A drowsy cricket faintly strummed,
And far away a partridge drummed

In secret code—and only I
Was silent now. Across the sky
Bright syllables were piped by birds;
A chipmunk chattered piquant words.

We humans are so very vain . . .
I heard at twilight's misty wane
Small creatures speak within the wood,
And not one word I understood.

Ruth B. Field

Photo Opposite
SUGAR HOUSE
LOWER WATERFORD, VT
Dick Smith

Gingham

Gingham always seems to me
A fabric spun of history.
I see a red-checked cloth hold food
Of patient love, of fortitude.
I watch a candle's loveliness
Lighting a small girl's Sunday dress.
It was so durable, so plain,
And yet, against a windowpane

Its common cheerful blue and white
Filled sober eyes with brief delight,
And sometimes it was edged with lace
To light a trusting little face.
Linen can give a heart a lift,
Shimmering silk is beauty's gift,
Proud velvet makes a royal show,
But gingham sings of long ago!

Geraldine Ross

Patchwork

It takes more than saying
to make love so.
It takes being and doing
as stitch by stitch
Love makes a pattern
that endures.

Marilou Awiakta

Appalachia

Lord, give me homespun and velvet,
bricks and pearls,
roses and a twist of lemon.
Homespun for virtue and velvet
for pleasure,
bricks for building and pearls
for pondering,
love and a twist of humor
for my soul.

Marilou Awiakta

Abiding Appliachia: Where Mountain and Atom Meet, by Marilou Awiakta. St. Luke's Press, copyright© 1978.
Used by permission of the publisher.

Just Before Bedtime

Each night when shadows gather
And we have climbed the stairs,
My mother reads a book to us
Before we say our prayers.

Sometimes she lets me
    choose the page—
I know the words by heart.
I always snuggle close to dad,
Way past the scary part.

The others have their
    favorites, too—
Tom loves the
    flying horse.
Our book is filled
    with pictures;
Mom lets us look,
    of course.

Our Nation's Homes

By its homes one knows a nation,
Not its wisdom or its wealth,
And their strength in true relation
Shows the nature of its health.

'Round the hearthstone, almost holy,
Met the families of yore
As they worshipped God who solely
Guided every hope and chore.

In its homes this land was nourished
By the Bible and by bread
Till its minds and souls both flourished,
And its hearts were duly fed.

There regard was born for neighbors.
There respect for elders dwelt.
There was respite from one's labors.
There concern for each was felt.

From its homes came wholesome thinking
That has made this country great,
Down the generations linking
To each other by this trait.

May our homes accept their duty
In the future as the past,
Giving strength and inner beauty
That allow a land to last.

Margaret Rorke

My Rural Heritage

I'm thankful for my heritage,
For fields of ripening grain,
For nature's special gifts to man
Of sun and wind and rain.

I'm thankful for the rooster's call
To summon us to day,
For doves that coo at evening time
In such a gentle way.

I love the fields of summer corn,
The scent of fresh-cut hay.
I love the setting August sun—
A fire at close of day.

I'm thankful for my heritage
Where neighbors work together,
Where each man helps his fellowman
In every kind of weather.

I love the rich and fertile soil
Of which I am a part.
I love the grand communion
Of deeply thankful hearts.

The hills to roam, the country school,
The creeks to wade and fish
Unite to form a heritage
As grand as one could wish.

Craig E. Sathoff

Inherit the Earth

Have you ever climbed to a mountaintop
And gazed at the valley below,
Or heard the deep roar on an ocean shore
When the gales and the tempests blow?

Ice caps and glaciers, forests and farms,
The rivers, the lakes, and the streams,
Cities and hamlets from coast to coast—
This is the land of your dreams.

Flowers and fruits, the sweet-singing birds,
Rhythm of darkness and day,
From the clouds in the sky to the depths of the sea,
What marvels there are on display!

You inherit the earth. Its wonders are yours,
So rise up and stretch your arms wide.
Let your heart sing exultantly, "This land is mine
To behold and to cherish with pride."

Mary A. Selden

Our Heritage

From the time the Pilgrims landed
And heard the wild Indians yell,
To the ride of Paul Revere
And the sound of the Liberty Bell,

We have followed our traditions
Changing plans that were not right.
We have scaled the highest mountains
And discovered the ocean's might.

We have seen the buffalo vanish,
Had our young men called to arms;
We have made this wonderful country,
Built her bridges, and loved her charms.

When you travel over the desert
To the white and sandy shore,
Remember this is your heritage
From our fathers in times of yore.

Polly Perkins

Goin' Home

Goin' home—what lovelier word
  Ever—ever—could be heard,
Home to warmth and firelight,
  Little rooms that shine at night,
Back to the comfort of old things,
  A kitchen where a kettle sings.

Goin' home—to supper spread,
  Fried potatoes and homemade bread,
Slippers warm beside the hearth,
  Loveliest spot in all the earth,
A new book and an easy chair,
  Someone precious waiting there.

Goin' home—to the place you've made
  With your own hands that you wouldn't trade
For a palace on a golden hill;
  Where you've sweated and planned until
Every tree in the rooted soil
  Is yours by dint of patient toil.

Goin' home—with heart aglow,
  Down the old road white with snow.
There a lighted window gleams,
  Sending out its golden beams
Like a lighthouse tall and white,
  Shining out against the night.

Goin' home—what lovelier word
Ever—ever—has been heard?

Edna Jaques

Photo Opposite
DWIGHT-BARNARD HOUSE
DEERFIELD, MA
Fred Sieb

On the Road
to Home...

Close of Day

A little road leads to home
At close of day
Where lighted windows beckon you
To come and stay.
And when you step within the door,
Your heart finds rest
In sharing joy or cares with those
You love the best.

Hilda Butler Farr

Silhouettes

All along the evening road
Lovely silhouettes I see,
Steeples etched against the sky,
Here and there a giant tree;

But the one that warms my heart
As I turn in at the gate
Shows a room with firelight
Where my loved ones wait.

Mildred S. Ferguson

Home

The road by which I come at night
Winds through a woodland green
And climbs a magic hillside
Where small fairies have been seen.
Oh, there are perfumed vales and dells
Through which my footsteps wend
Before I reach the cottage home
That waits at journey's end.
But I see not the summer flow'rs
That bloom in sweet array;
I hurry so to reach my home,
I hardly note the way.

Brian F. King

That Crooked Road to Home

A picture from a scrapbook old,
I ran across today;
A picture of a crooked road
Where shadows softly play;
A road that seemed so friendly and
A road that beckoned you,
Extending invitation to
Explore a vista new.

There, flanking it on either side,
A row of maple trees
Were just the backdrop for a stage
Where nature was at ease.
And where it narrowed just a bit,
There stood a covered bridge
That partly hid the beauty of
A blossom-sheltered ridge.

That picture meant so much to me
And held intent my gaze,
While mind was empty but for scene
Portrayed of other days.
It fostered longing in my heart,
A longing just to roam,
With memory as companion down
That crooked road to home.

Fred Toothaker

Photo Overleaf
THE ROAD TO HOME
SOUTH WOODSTOCK, VT
Gene Ahrens

Hills of Home

Though I travel far in other lands
O'er billows of ocean foam,
There constantly lingers in my mind
The thoughts of the hills of home.

Other places have many beauties,
Wherever my footsteps roam,
But never anything weans my heart
From the rugged hills of home.

Though often I find myself tempted
To stray far 'neath God's blue dome,
Ever present is the keen yearning
For sight of the hills of home.

Adventure beckons me to wander,
To visit Paris and Rome,
But no matter where I chance to be
I long for the hills of home.

For many years I have wished to go
To the Yukon and to Nome,
But if I were there I know I'd long
For my dear-loved hills of home.

As the years roll on and take their toll,
No longer my footsteps roam,
But dear to my heart are memories
Of the rugged hills of home.

Myrtie Fisher Seaverns

Harvest Gold

Harvesttime brings riches,
Wealth of varied gold,
All the warmth of summer
Heaped against the cold.

Crispy, juicy apples
Of right-for-eating yellow,
Orange-red persimmons,
And pears gold and mellow.

Sweet corn nuggets
To delight hungry eyes,
And great orange pumpkins
For spice-brown pies.

Harvesttime is brimming
With all the bins can hold,
Foods for winter spending
In rich, ripe gold!

Esther York Burkholder

Painting Opposite
PICKING THE BEST
Richard Hook

Thanksgiving on the Farm

Thanksgiving is a time of year
When everyone is free from fear.
The cribs are loaded down with grain;
The cellar's stocked with garden gain.
The barn's prepared for winter storm;
The house is comfortable and warm.

And, best of all, the family's home.
Though some of them may like to roam
To places strange and far away,
They come back to the farm today.

They gather here with gratitude
For everything—each other, food,
Memories shared with Mom and Dad,
For health, and the success they've had.

Praising God's kind will at length,
They find an extra meed of strength,
Renewal for the work of living
Through this ritual of Thanksgiving!

Bertha Garland

Thankfulness

To thank for a season
Of rest between
Autumn and springtime's
Beautiful scene,
For a storehouse full
When summer departs,
For wholesome pleasures
That cheer our hearts.

To thank for friends
Who help us bear
With patience daily
Each trifling care,
Who lend a hand in
Time of distress
In true concern for
Our happiness.

To thank for a country
Great and free,
Its leaders, our homes
And liberty,
Courage to soften us
To our foes,
In love till the world
With peace o'erflows.

To make a glorious
Day complete,
To make each hour
Full and sweet,
To thank the Lord for
Life worth living—
That is the real and
True Thanksgiving.

Abigail Falk

Thanksgiving: Past Imperfect

We recently moved away from kith and kin and relocated in a community hundreds of miles from anywhere we'd ever been before. When Thanksgiving came around, we were invited by some new friends to join them and several other upwardly-mobile young couples for a holiday dinner—adults only. It was an evening to remember. The table was set with an exquisite arrangement of spicy gold chrysanthemums and autumn leaves. Bone china and lead crystal gleamed between flatware of shimmering sterling. Crisp linen underlined the settings and crowned each plate. In the serene glow of flickering tapers, we dined on a gourmet menu which included chilled cream of broccoli soup, Cornish game hens in nests of wild rice, artichoke hearts vinaigrette and—the grand finale—praline bananas en flambé. It was utterly perfect—too perfect. In fact, it was hardly recognizable as Thanksgiving.

For me, Thanksgiving has always been a holiday full of family, confusion, craziness, and characters. It's the one holiday based on two principles that defy packaging or perfection. The whole day revolves around gratitude and eating—not necessarily in that order. We're talking about the basics here and when a family gathers together and gets down to basics, strange things happen.

First of all, there are always more people than room. This means innovative seating arrangements must be devised. We always started with a large sheet of plywood on top of the dining room table. This usually created as many problems as it solved. We could seat extra folks, but the tablecloths never quite fit and the table was so wide and long, it was difficult to reach things. Then there was the droop factor. If the plywood was much larger than the table top, it took on a sort of convex appearance where the edges were a bit lower than the center. This was all right until Uncle Fred decided to hunker down with both elbows to get a better purchase on a drumstick. On one such occasion, the creamed onions gave into gravity and slid gracefully into Grandma's lap.

Children were always a prerequisite at Thanksgiving. If they were under two they were usually perched on telephone books or in high chairs next to a tolerant relative in washable clothes. From this vantage, the little

darlings could, and usually did, pitch everything from salad to creamed peas with alarming accuracy. EFO's (edible flying objects) were always a part of every Thanksgiving I can recall.

If you were over two, but under fourteen, you were obliged to occupy a card table. One leg always threatened to cave in if nudged properly. The best thing about being at a card table, however, was the location—usually in the living room or a spare bedroom and out of earshot of any adults. You could burp, reach across the table, stick pitted olives on all ten fingers, or tell a joke with equal impunity. Someone always got the giggles right after taking a drink of milk and, depending upon the degree of muscle control, more or less saturated things. It was great! "Tell us the one about the school teacher with the hives again, Harold!"

Table settings were eclectic. No one knew it was called that, but that's what it was. Whoever had enough dishes and silverware for 25 people? The grown-ups got the good things that matched. The older children got the everyday stuff, but might end up with a salad fork and a tablespoon because the regular size was used up. Little people got divided plastic picnic plates and plastic glasses. The only crystal around was in Aunt Edna's brooch. The "good silver" really wasn't. It was plate, in a pattern called Queen Anne's Lace, and had been purchased with an astronomical number of Betty Crocker coupons.

The Thanksgiving menu was fairly predictable: turkey, candied sweet potatoes, mashed potatoes and gravy, creamed onions, peas and carrots, a fruit salad, dressing, relishes, and pies for dessert. Lots of pies. Everyone brought part of the dinner and it was assembled at the host's home. This usually made for some interesting developments—like the year Aunt Mildred's individual gelatin turkeys melted in the backseat during a traffic jam. I won't relate what the end product looked like, but cousin Ellen's description made for great hilarity and lots of sprayed milk at one of the card tables.

Each relative had a "specialty" item, and it was prepared with great pride and received with appreciation—usually. Aunt Katie, however, always tried to be innovative. One year she experimented with horseradish in the aspic to "spice it up" as she said. She did a bang-up job! On another occasion she developed a variation of the classic perfection salad that henceforth was known as "Katie's imperfection." At least she always added an element of surprise to the day.

The only time we ever had anything "en flambé" was the year Uncle Ben discovered a recipe in some magazine for doing the turkey in a brown paper bag. That was the same year we spent an hour trying to explain to Great-Grandma that we realized it wasn't traditional to have hot dogs on Thanksgiving.

Gratitude was always an integral part of our family gatherings and everyone was expected to share at least one blessing from the past year. Often, these testimonials were touching, sometimes heartwarming, always interesting and, on occasion, questionable. One that sticks in my memory was the year Uncle Harry rose solemnly, held up his water goblet, and intoned prayerfully, "I am extremely grateful that my beloved sister, Ada, has seen fit to spare us from her asparagus crepes this Thanksgiving." He sat down to a chorus of "Amens" and a patient sigh from Ada as she passed this year's offering, zucchini strata.

At our Thanksgiving dinners, the guests were as mis-matched as the china. Uncle Richard, a nuclear engineer, chatted amicably with the young gas station attendant who had married one of the cousins. A first-time mother conferred with Great-Grandma about the ageless concerns of colic and cradle-cap. The children, all shapes and sizes, fit into all the niches—empty laps, empty corners, empty arms. It was a holiday that was warm, unstructured, and held together with the adhesive that binds us still—love.

Reflecting now upon it all, I must admit that my new friends' Thanksgiving was delicious and beautiful and wonderfully perfect. But I think if I could choose, I'd opt for my Thanksgivings—past-imperfect. For despite the chaos and confusion, they were always perfectly wonderful.

Pamela Kennedy

I Would Give Thanks

I would give thanks for many things
On this Thanksgiving Day,
Thanks for all the blessings life brings
Each day along the way.

I would give thanks for life, for health,
For home, for food, and too,
All that I count my greatest wealth . . .
Family and friendships true.

I give thanks for my native land,
For freedom on this day,
Where we worship and understand
Our privilege to pray.

I would give thanks for many things
And do the best I can
To be worthy of all life brings
And serve my fellowman.

Virginia Katherine Oliver

Photo Opposite
GIVING THANKS
Fred Sieb

The Mayflower

There is a peace that harbors here
Where silver waves come murmuring
Against the quaint, old-weathered pier
Where a host of memories cling.
A brave old ship lies in repose
Where it is anchored safe at last.
Along the gold and amber shore,
It reminisces of the past.

Through the years' remembering,
It sees again the Pilgrim band
And knows anew their trials and tears,
Their yearning for a bright new land.
It braves the stormy seas that roar,
The wind that howls its cry of doom
And hears the feeble voices sing
Their hymns of praise amidst the gloom.

Through the seas that rise and swell,
It bears the dauntless little band
Across the wide and perilous blue
To a far and distant land . . .
And still the waves come murmuring,
Within the hour a silence clings,
Where an old ship lies at anchor now
With but the glory of a dream.

Joy Belle Burgess

Heritage

The Pilgrims left their distant shores
To find a better life,
To have a home where freedom reigned,
But they faced want and strife.

The untamed land was filled with fears
For those who came that day,
Yet still those brave and struggling folks
Made up their minds to stay.

They faced the fears and tamed the land,
And made a homeland here.
They bravely met and conquered strife
And held their new home dear.

Our heritage is strong and grand,
Sincere and fine and true.
We're thankful for the Pilgrim folks
And proud of our land too.

Lois Anne Williams

Thanksgiving

More intricate and more complex
Than the lives our Pilgrim fathers had,
Our years are spent with much to vex
And much to make us glad.
But just as they paused to pray,
We pause to thank Thee, God, today.

The sun was theirs, the sun is ours.
The good earth yields as it did then.
We have the same life-giving showers.
We have the women and the men
Who have walked bravely through the years,
Facing and conquering their fears.

We have the bounty of our land;
We thank Thee, God, that we are blessed.
In countless ways thy outflung hand
Has given us what has been best.
Accept the praise that each heart lifts,
And make us worthy of thy gifts.

Grace Noll Crowell

Photo Opposite
CHURCH IN THE VILLAGE GREEN
TOWNSHEND, VT
Dick Smith

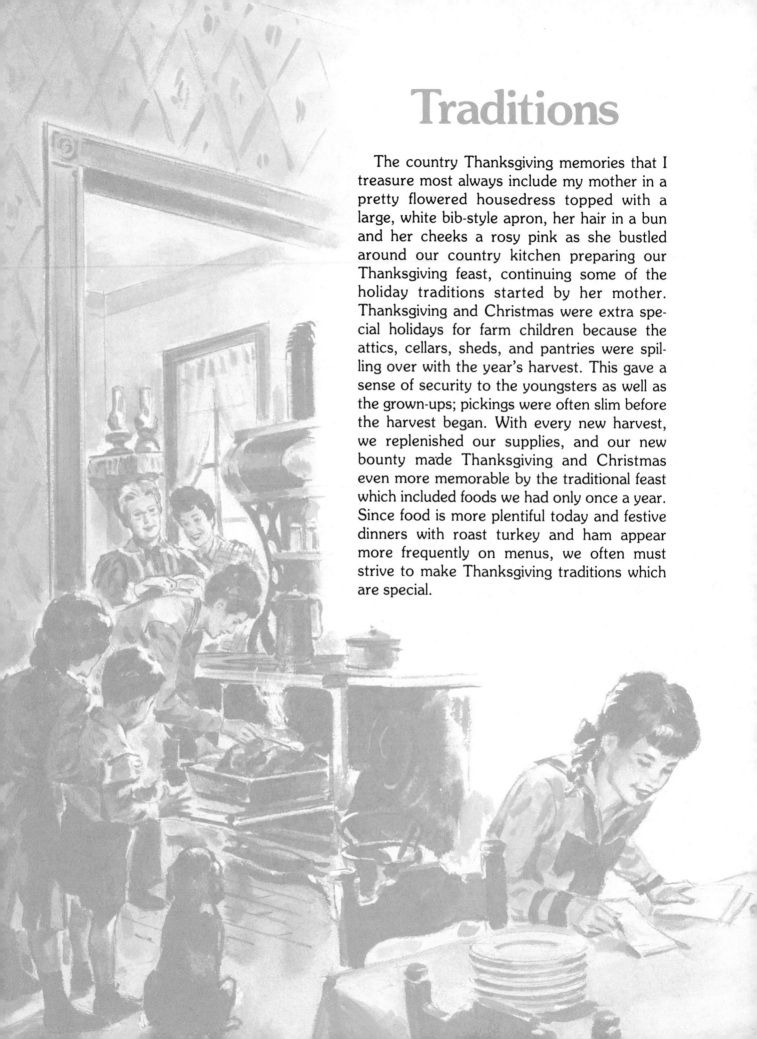

Traditions

The country Thanksgiving memories that I treasure most always include my mother in a pretty flowered housedress topped with a large, white bib-style apron, her hair in a bun and her cheeks a rosy pink as she bustled around our country kitchen preparing our Thanksgiving feast, continuing some of the holiday traditions started by her mother. Thanksgiving and Christmas were extra special holidays for farm children because the attics, cellars, sheds, and pantries were spilling over with the year's harvest. This gave a sense of security to the youngsters as well as the grown-ups; pickings were often slim before the harvest began. With every new harvest, we replenished our supplies, and our new bounty made Thanksgiving and Christmas even more memorable by the traditional feast which included foods we had only once a year. Since food is more plentiful today and festive dinners with roast turkey and ham appear more frequently on menus, we often must strive to make Thanksgiving traditions which are special.

Down on the farm where I live today, we don't mind the "extras" which keep Thanksgivings as special as they were in Mom's day. We reserve roast turkey, dressing, and all of the trimmings for our Thanksgiving Day feast. Thanksgiving is still a family day, with all the kinfolk gathered around a large dining room table to give special thanks for our most bountiful feast of the year. Much of our food is still raised on the farm, keeping us aware of how blessed we are to have it. I find myself following in my mother's footsteps as we carry on the holiday traditions which Mom's family had passed down to her. I treasure them, and my daughter has discovered that she, too, must observe Thanksgiving traditions the way her own mother has always done.

For a time, we went modern down on the farm—out went the old wood stoves, pantries, butter churns, rocking chairs, and most anything that was classified as old-fashioned. Since then, many of us have come to our senses and long for a cozy country kitchen. Now we have a kitchen more like Mom's to prepare this year's Thanksgiving Day feast. I want my Thanksgiving to be memorable and traditional with a black wood stove to hover over as I cook the same old-fashioned specialties my mother did. By following these long-established traditions, we've found the secret to a perfect Thanksgiving, an old-fashioned holiday observation—with a dash or two of modernity—which is a happy combination of new and old traditions to please us all.

Helen Colwell Oakley

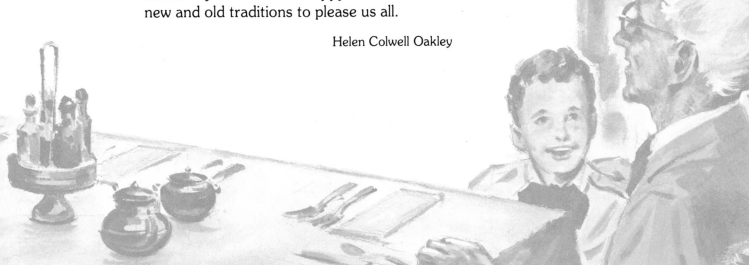

Thanksgiving Day

There's a sound of merry laughter
Pealing out from down the lane,
And the bells on horses' bridles
Make a happy noise again.

The turkey's in the oven,
Roasting to a golden brown;
The table's fixed so ten or twelve
Or more can sit around.

The pumpkin and the mincemeat pies
Cool temptingly nearby;
The house smells spicy and fragrant-sweet
From flaky, fresh-baked pie.

The noise is growing louder,
There's loud stomping now of feet!
The door swings wide and voices shout,
"Hi, folks! We're starved! When do we eat?"

Silence fills the dear old house,
Each member bows his head
As Father thanks the Lord above
For such a bounteous spread.

Then the sound of merry laughter
Fills the house with joy and play . . .
Oh, it's grand to be with those you love
And share Thanksgiving Day.

Mrs. Paul E. King

Painting Opposite
JUST IN TIME
John Walter

Thanksgiving

Mindful of the blessings
Which are given us to share,
We thank God on Thanksgiving
With a special, grateful prayer.

For the seasons with their beauty,
Each one a jewel so rare,
Bringing us much happiness
And peace beyond compare.

For every silver raindrop
And each golden ray of sun,
For the magic of the moon and stars
When each busy day is done.

We thank God for our loved ones
And the friendships that we know,
For the hills and fields and valleys
And our home with lamplight glow.

We feel an awe and wonder
When gazing at the trees,
That reach into the heavens
And talk to every breeze.

At the clouds so white and fleecy,
At the rainbow's wondrous spell,
And all of nature's creatures
Living in the woods and dell.

The rivers, streams, and oceans
That are gorgeous to behold
And every lovely flower
Which only come from God's mold.

We pray we may be worthy
Of God's faith and trust and love,
To do the best we can
When smiles come from above.

We can bear our pain and sorrow,
We can bear our cross 'tis true.
If Thanksgiving is within our hearts,
Hope is ever born anew.

Not only on Thanksgiving
Should we pray and grateful be,
But every day we live
For God is good to you and me.

LaVerne P. Larson

Photo Overleaf
NEW ENGLAND VILLAGE
Fred Sieb

Some Good to Do

If there's some good that I can do
To ease another's way,
If I can cause the sun to shine
Or moonbeams softly play,

If I can help to make a dream—
A lifelong dream come true,
My purpose for existing will
Be most rewarding, too.

If just a simple word of cheer
I might pass on to you,
Or help to ease a lonely hour
Of those whose friends are few,

Then I am rich for I have gained
A satisfaction sweet
In working out God's will for me
With all of those I meet.

I'd draw them into common bond
And for them daily pray;
I want to be God's instrument
To ease another's way.

Georgia B. Adams

Falling Leaves

When leaves are softly falling,
We hear them as they go,
Talking in a whisper
About the winter's snow.

And as they hunt for flowers,
Which need a warm bedspread,
They entertain by dancing
Around each flower bed.

Then trees can be heard singing
Their sweet yet lonesome songs
Until they know each leaflet
Has found where it belongs.

The leaves have served a purpose
From shiny new to old;
Their life, begun with greenness,
Now ends like flakes of gold.

Eva N. Ehrman

Lord, behold our family here assembled. We thank Thee for this place in which we dwell; for the love that unites us; for the peace accorded us this day; for the hope with which we expect the morrow.

ROBERT LOUIS STEVENSON

By All These Signs I Knew

Today, upon a gold-crowned hill,
I felt the first, faint, frosty chill;
A leaf fell softly at my feet
Where mellow apples, musty sweet,
Perfumed the languid, country air
And mingled with the scent of pear.
A redwing spurned his spring-built nest
And disappeared into the west.
Rose petals scattered on the ground
To cover up an earthy mound
That housed a sleepy, blinking toad,
While dust-whirls circled down the road.
Scarecrows, lately spruce and neat,
Drooped wearily in stubbled wheat.
By all these signs I knew, I knew,
Jack Frost was stirring Winter's brew.

Emily Carey Alleman

Jack Frost's Dream

One evening Jack Frost, in a terrible grouch,
Lay down to sleep on his three-feather couch.
"No one's aware of what I go through,"
He said to himself as he pulled off one shoe.
"Nobody knows about all of the work
That it takes on this job, and I never would shirk.

"When the trees are all painted with colors so deep,
The bear knows it's time for a long winter's sleep.
The farmer must hurry and gather the corn
So the cattle can eat on a cold winter morn.
Besides being useful, it's pretty, I claim.
The folks from the city all rave and exclaim,

"But they don't appreciate just what I do.
They ought to be forced to get somebody new."
With these very words he fell into his bed,
And then a strange dream came into his head.
He made up his mind he was going to retire;
He'd contract his work, some elves he would hire.

He knew some who painted the flowers of spring.
He picked up his phone and gave them a ring.
They accepted his offer for a reasonable fee
(Not one of them had ever painted a tree).
Jack walked in the woods the very next day,
And all that he saw filled his heart with dismay.

The maple was painted a bright gentian blue,
And the elm tree was wearing a purplish hue.
The brightest of pink was the sturdy old birch.
The magpie was speechless on a lavender perch.
Said Jack, "This must be some terrible joke."
The alarm rang loud and then he awoke.

It was four in the morning, a very good hour
To start with his painting on each leaf and bower.
He sang as he worked and whistled a tune,
And spoke these wise words to the man in the moon:
"When you can do something that needs to be done,
Be happy to do it, it really is fun."

Emily Preputin

Painted Leaves of Autumn

The painted leaves of autumn,
In their flaming, blazing show,
Pave the way to tomorrow
With winter's drifting snow.

As the last leaf flutters
To eternal rest below,
The earth quietly awaits
The first falling of snow.

The painted leaves of autumn
Fling banners on every tree.
And I eagerly await the day
Winter's snow will fall on me.

Lucille Crumley

Marian Lorraine Moore

Marian L. Moore was born and educated in Salem, Oregon. After a high school teacher encouraged her writing, Ms. Moore worked harder at her poetry and started selling her work to magazines. Her poems have been published in such diverse periodicals as *The Capitol Journal*, *The Oregon Journal*, *Midwest Horizons*, *The Country Bard*, *Now*, and *The Young People's Journal*.

Ms. Moore has a strong pioneer heritage (her grandfather was a stagecoach driver) and this is often reflected in her poetic expressions of a firm faith and love of country. *ideals®* has featured the poetry of Marian Moore for many years, and we are pleased to present her as *Thanksgiving's* Best-Loved Poet.

Thank You, God

Another year has come and gone.
On this Thanksgiving Day,
O God, our hearts are turned to thee;
With grateful thanks we pray.

For all thy care which shelters us
Wherever we may go,
For wonders of thy bounteous love
Which ever make it so,

For all the beauties of the world
Created by thy hand
And given to your people here
Who dwell upon the land,

For harvest when the autumn flings
Her color to the sky,
For winter silence, soft and deep,
Protecting snow, piled high,

For all thy wondrous gifts to us,
Your children here below,
We offer grateful thanks to thee;
Our love for you will grow.

It's the Little Things I Cherish

It's the little things I cherish,
Just a walk along the beach
Or a squirrel which chatters gaily
A short distance beyond reach.

Something there for just a moment,
Single leaf of purest gold,
Heralding the autumn season
With the joys that it may hold.

Or that moment when the springtime
Cradles earth against her breast;
In a field of fragrant flowers,
There the tired world finds rest.

When the royal design of heaven
Shifts to patterns of the fall,
There in fond and loving memory
Lives a dream which I recall.

All these little things I cherish
As the year is hastening on,
Things to add to memory's pages
As the book is closed and gone.

Thanksgiving in the Country

The warmth of God's love at Thanksgiving
Surrounding His children on earth;
When minds are turning toward harvest,
With the spring to come, a new birth.

Fruits of the vine have been gathered in,
And barns for hard weather secured.
Summer has gone and autumn is here;
Quite soon winter will come for sure.

The season of growing has ended,
And farmers have brought the crops in.
The fields now lie empty and barren
Where abundant harvest had been.

Another year brought to fulfillment
Gives cause for the thankful to pray
And offer all praise to the Father,
Being faithful in every way.

The tables with good things are laden
With a promise to come of the feast.
All of the family enjoying,
From the greatest down to the least.

When all heads are bowed at the table
Then thanks are offered to God
For harvest so full He's provided,
Being given from our native sod.

The family gives praise for the blessings
God has showered down on each one.
The year quickly comes to its closing
Before yet another's begun.

Nightfall on the River

Swallows dip low to the water
As the sun begins its descent.
Trees near the bank of the river
Low to the water are bent.

Softly the wind in their branches
Singing a soft lullaby,
While evening falls on the river,
Sleepy birds utter their cry.

Last rays of sun on the water
Sparkle and dance in the light,
As silence reigns on the river,
Waiting arrival of night.

Twilight brings peace to the forest;
Sounds of the day disappear.
Night settles in with the darkness;
Rest for all creatures is near.

A sky full of stars is the ceiling
Spread o'er the scene down below.
Night softly falls on the river,
Feeling the peace as we go

Back to our lives in the city,
Where responsibilities call,
But never forgetting the river
As end of day brought nightfall.

A Prayer at Thanksgiving

Dear Lord, as autumn drops across the land,
A crisp reminder of chilly days ahead,
The sight of falling leaves on every hand,
And hillsides etched in sparkling gold and red—

We ask thy guidance for the family here.
Our work, receive all blessings from above,
That we may have a most successful year.
Give us your grace and ever constant love.

Keep us forever in a watchful glow
And may we never fail to do thy will;
So looking down upon us here below,
Our hearts with all your heavenly peace fulfill.

This is our prayer, that we may spread the light
Of truth to all who labor in thy sight.

Photo Overleaf
FIRST SNOW
INTERVALE, NH
Fred Sieb

Last Days of Autumn

Guess who left his calling card
On leaves of red and gold,
And on the grass, a brittle shard
Of glassy ice so cold?
None other than Jack Frost, who came
To visit in the night,
Wrapped in a sheet of freezing rain,
A portent of his might.

Fresh logs are by the fireplace
And will send forth a rosy glow
Of pleasant warmth on hands and face
When ground is white with snow.
In Grandma's cellar you will find
On shelves all trim and neat,
Her home preserves of every kind
For a coming winter's treat.

The storm doors are already in,
And shutters fastened tight;
Coal and wood are in the bin
For winter is in sight.

Elsie Natalie Brady

Fall to Winter

The autumn leaves of red and gold
Fall gently to the ground,
As robins and their feathered friends
Are quickly southward bound.

The trees upon the hillside
In every radiant hue,
Soon will shed their leaves to earth
For winter's rendezvous.

The morning air gives off a chill
As fall slowly declines,
While Jack Frost paints on windowpanes
His intricate designs.

Time will pass, the limbs will bare,
And fall will pass on by
As sparkling flakes of snowy white
Fall softly from the sky.

Linn E. Nolen

Celebrate Christmas with *ideals*®

What is your favorite Christmas memory? Do you still carry on holiday traditions started by your parents or grandparents? We invite you to join us as *ideals*® remembers some well-loved traditions in our next issue, *Christmas ideals*®.

As we count our holiday blessings here at *ideals*®, we are thankful for our faithful readers, like Judy Rybarczyk of Stevens Point, Wisconsin, who writes:

> I think the folks at Ideals Publishing really have a way of doing nice things for their subscribers! After having received my first eight (out of a total of sixteen) editions of *ideals*®, I easily perceive how very much you appreciate your readers!
>
> The evidence for this assertion is found cover to cover, on every page—a rainbow of color, seasonal commentary; vibrant color, poetry; magnificent color, inspiring material; joyful color, patriotic themes; bright and beautiful color, nostalgic themes; uplifting color, humor— and the proof goes on into the future.
>
> Furthermore, I have recognized this standard of quality that is consistently praiseworthy after purchasing, for many years, past copies of Christmas and Easter *ideals*® .... I am grateful for your excellent planning of each *ideals*® issue. I must offer a heartfelt *"Thank You"* because you surely deserve it!

Thank *you*, Ms. Rybarczyk! We *do* appreciate *all* our readers, and hope all of you have a Happy Thanksgiving and a very Merry Christmas season.

ACKNOWLEDGEMENTS

THANKSGIVING by Grace Noll Crowell, used by permission of the Estate of Grace Noll Crowell; GOIN' HOME by Edna Jaques from her book *HILLS OF HOME*, copyright© 1946 by Thomas Allen Publishers, Ltd. Our sincere thanks to the following authors whose addresses we were unable to locate: the Estate of Mildred S. Ferguson for SILHOUETTES from her book *VOICE AT THE CROSS ROAD*; Bertha Garland for THANKSGIVING ON THE FARM; the Estate of Brian F. King for HOME; Kirstin for FAIRY SHIPS; Linn E. Nolen for FALL TO WINTER; Geraldine Ross for GINGHAM: the Estate of Myrtie Fisher Seaverns for HILLS OF HOME from her book *THE HILLS OF HOME;* and Andrea Kerry Shafer for RED ROSES.